God Is Building A House

God Is Building A House

Sylvia Mary Alison

Marshalls

Marshalls Paperbacks
Marshall Morgan & Scott
3 Beggarwood Lane, Basingstoke, Hants RG23 7LP, UK

First published by Marshall Morgan & Scott Ltd. 1984

ISBN 0551 01161 0

Typeset by Ann Buchan (Typesetters)
Surrey
Printed in Great Britain by Anchor Brendon Ltd,
Tiptree, Essex.

Contents

To Michael, my beloved husband
and to our children
James, Sebastian and Mary Rose
with gratitude for their love and forbearance.

All royalties for this book will go to Prison Fellowship England and Wales, P. 0. Box 263, London SW1

Foreword

I live with the author of this book. We have been married for 26 years. During most of this time she has had to travel on one of the most difficult of all married pilgrimages: that of a parliamentarian's wife. It is no life for a contemplative. She has had to accommodate herself to two homes, one in London, the other in my constituency. Both had to be lived in regularly and actively; and unlike the pleasures involved in possessing second or holiday homes, ceaseless travel between these two bases—often alone but for our young children—involved years of emotional and physical strain. Then she has had to accommodate herself to loneliness. The parliamentarian's working day tends to start at the same time as everybody else's, but to stretch late into the evening. How often has my wife had to sit alone at home, waiting for my late return from the House of Commons, unable to go out on her own account because of the ties of a young family! Then she has had to accommodate herself to endless practical duties of the sort often performed by a husband: driving the car long distances on her own; at home and abroad; organising and supervising repairs and maintenance in the two homes; interviewing headmasters and headmistresses for the children's schooling, and so on—all occasioned by the peculiar demands which parliamentary, and especially ministerial life place upon husbands with full time jobs in Whitehall and Westminster, but with constituencies far away from London.

The glimpse which my wife gives in this book into her inner life and spirit—and more, into that limitless dimension which feeds it—is thus a glimpse into a life stretched outwardly with activity, responsibility and strain. It has not been a life which afforded the time or the inclination for idle fantasies. Although more cerebral than my wife in our shared faith, I can testify that what she writes about is real—for both of us. For my own parliamentary and ministerial life would have been quite impossible, particularly in relation to the occasions of disappointment, strain and illness which affect us all, if the indomitable spirit of faith and hope in her frail body had not provided enough for both of us, and kept the ship afloat.

Michael Alison

Introduction

This book is written in the form of a personal testimony. It is basically a call to prayer, a call to Christians to get to know their Lord in a more personal way, and to co-operate with Him in His purposes in the world. On the one hand it is a call to closer discipleship and obedience—part of God's preparation of the Bride for the Marriage Feast of the Lamb—and on the other hand an attempt to show God at work, as I see it, in renewing and recreating the structures of society according to His holiness and righteousness. It is also about the birth of Prison Fellowship in England and Wales. And it is a book about organic growth, as opposed to organisational structures.

I wrote the book because John Hunt, now the Managing Director of Marshall Pickering, asked me to do so. He had heard one or two tapes of talks I had given to Lydia Conferences, and he asked me to write down in book form what I said at meetings. Practically everything in this book I have already spoken out at some meeting or another. Chapters 8, 9, and 11 are taken directly from two tapes spoken at Lydia Conferences in 1981, one in May in Swanick, and one in June in Hove.

I have kept to a certain theme in this book and so naturally have not spoken much about the day to day details of our life. But I am deeply conscious of how much I have failed to be for my children the sort of mother they deserved—each of them so very special, and each deserving far more care and attention than I, with my other preoccupations, ever managed to give them.

There are so many people that I am so grateful to and should thank for so many things, that I don't know where to begin. But I would just like to mention our Monday intercession group, Gwenda Hordern, Audrey Metters, Jane Bretherton, Vivian Sewell (who also typed my manuscript) Jennet Kidd, the late Romany White Abbott, LaDonna Elliott, and an infrequent comer, but very important, Jean Darnall. Together we have learned, week by week, to listen to our Lord, bind up each others hurts and wounds, and worship Him. And to know a depth of friendship that is very precious.

Sylvia Mary Alison

1

Learning to listen

The first time that I became aware of hearing the Holy Spirit speaking was way back in the autumn of 1954. Youth for Christ were holding a series of rallies on Saturday evenings at the Central Hall, Westminster, and on each Saturday they invited two Billy Graham converts to give their testimonies. Billy Graham had held his famous three month crusade at Harringay Arena earlier that year, and in the first week of March I had gone forward at the close of a meeting to commit my life to Christ. That spring I was doing the London Season as a debutante, being presented at court, going to Queen Charlotte's Ball and several of the parties that the Season entailed in those days, and I suppose the rally organisers wanted a contrast in their testimonies, because they asked me to speak with a barrow boy who, as a result of his conversion, was going to be ordained.

My bible class teacher suggested I pray for a verse of scripture to focus my comments that evening. I had never spoken at a meeting before, and was very nervous. For days I prayed and thought, and the only verse that came to my mind was Acts 1:8: 'But ye shall receive power after that the Holy Ghost is come upon you, and ye shall be witnesses unto me both in Jerusalem, in Judaea, in Samaria and unto the uttermost part of the earth.' Baffled, I tried to push the verse away and think of something else. I couldn't. So then I tried to think of something relevant to me that fitted in with the verse. I couldn't think of anything. Finally, I arrived at the Central Hall at the appointed time in a flat panic. I hadn't the faintest idea what I was going to say, and was merely armed with this apparently irrelevant verse which I couldn't think what to do with.

The Centrall Hall was full. I sat on the platform with what seemed an army of men in dog collars, and the only comforting presence was that of the barrow boy, who appeared to be just as nervous as I was. As the evening went on I became more and more fearful, till the only thing I was conscious of was the loud and painful beating of my heart.

Suddenly, breaking into my panic, came a still small voice. 'Don't be afraid,' the voice said. 'You will be brought before kings and governors for my name's sake. You don't need to think what to say. It will be given you in that hour what you shall speak.'

Calmed and intrigued I listened. What kings? What governors? I was so fascinated by what God was going to do, that I stopped being scared. When it came to my turn to move to the microphone, I was interviewed by one of the clergymen, who asked me questions. Suddenly Acts 1 : 8 became relevant in answer to one of his questions, so I quoted it. The whole interview can have taken no more than about five minutes. If I'd had a speech prepared I would have had to scrap it, so it's just as well I hadn't. Thankfully I sat down and enjoyed the rest of the evening.

A few days later I received a letter from one of the clergymen. He said that more people had come forward to receive Christ at the end of that meeting than at any other Youth for Christ rally in that series, and it had been through my testimony. Amazed, I stared at the letter. It was awesome. How could anyone have come to Christ through those few disjointed sentences that I couldn't even recall? It was clearly nothing to do with me. 'God's ways are not our ways.'

When I was asked to write this book, I didn't really know at first what it was going to be about. But as I wrote, the main theme that emerged seemed to me to be about learning to listen to God, to recognise the voice of the Holy Spirit.

I would like, in this book to show you how God has brought to pass the things he showed me that evening when I was eighteen years old, but it was many years before they happened. Jesus says 'My sheep hear my voice,' and 'they know my voice'. He calls his disciples not servants, but friends. Friends are people who share secrets with one another. If I try to confide in a friend and that friend doesn't understand me, then I withdraw and talk of more superficial matters. So it is with our Lord. He longs to communicate with his disciples, to share his thoughts with them so that we may co-operate with him in his work in the world.

In the mid 1960s I learned this lesson most vividly. My husband is a Member of Parliament, and anyone who knows anything about the life of parliamentarians knows that MPs' wives see very little of their husbands, as the House of Commons sits every afternoon and evening. Throughout the '60s my children were little, and after they went to bed I had many lonely evenings while my husband was out working. I found the loneliness very difficult to take, and would often sink into deep depressions, sometimes lying on my bed and staring at the ceiling for hours, beyond tears. During the day, I'd always had groups of women coming to our flat for bible study. In the evenings I would often telephone one or other of these woman, thinking that I might talk to her and encourage her in her Christian life.

One day, as I was about to pick up the receiver to make such a call, I again sensed the Lord's presence and had a check in my spirit. 'You're not ringing her up to help her, you're ringing her up because you can't bear to be alone.' I paused, considering this thought, and realising that I had been kidding myself. 'But you are not alone: I am with you: I am your husband: talk to me.' I turned away from the telephone, bemused. 'I don't want to be rude, Lord, but I don't think I could talk to you for the whole evening. For half an hour perhaps, but longer than that. . . ?' However, I thought I would try it. I walked back into the sitting room, and sat in a chair pretending that Jesus was in the chair opposite. And then I started, consciously, but silently to talk to him.

Over a period of time I discovered many things. If you are having a conversation with someone, you shouldn't do all the talking. In order for the conversation to be a dialogue,both people need to talk and listen to each other. Otherwise they won't hear the other's point of view. I soon realised that in my conversations with God I was carrying on a monologue, telling him what I wanted and what I thought about things, but not asking him what he thought. After a time I dried up and couldn't think of anything else to say, so I began to ask him what he thought. Amazingly, new thoughts came into my mind, bits of scripture that I'd never considered before opened up to me. I soon found that for these conversations I needed a bible beside me to look things up. Another thing I learned was that if you love someone, you don't have to talk, or be talked to, all the time. You can just sit in silence and enjoy each other's company. 'In your presence is fullness of joy, at your right hand there are pleasures for evermore' (Psalm 16 : 11).

On one occasion, about eight years later, I discovered how much the Lord had taught me. By this time my children were at boarding school, so I was alone during the day as well as in the evenings. One particular week Michael was going to be out every evening except one. I was very excited about that one evening. I bought flowers for the drawing room, his favourite food for supper; I worked all day to make the evening a success. At about six o'clock he telephoned, his voice very disappointed. 'I'm so sorry, something has cropped up. I can't come home after all.' 'It's all right,' I said. 'It doesn't matter at all. I quite understand.' I'd said things like that before, really in order not to discourage Michael, but this time I found that I really meant it. I tried to prod my heart to see what had happened to that depression which would have engulfed me a few years before. But it wasn't there. I spent a very happy evening, in the sitting room with all those lovely flowers, doing nothing in particular, but I kept finding such joy welling up inside me that I could hardly contain it, and kept bursting into song. St Paul says: 'Not that I speak in respect of want, for I have learned in whatever state I am therewith to be content. I know how to be abased, and I know how to abound; in any and all circumstances I have learned the secret of facing plenty and hunger, abundance and want. I can do all things through him who strengthens me' (Phil. 4 : 11-13).

Jesus needs his disciples to be content in him, listening to his voice, and available for him to do what he wants with them: so that when we act we do things not out of our own needs, but in response to his requests and wishes. In this way Jesus, the head of the body, will be able to work through his body on earth.

2

A prophet to the nations

One day I was walking along the road to our local supermarket to buy groceries for the household. My mind was a jumble of food thoughts. What should we have for supper? What did I need to remember to buy? Quietly, but cutting through all my other thoughts by reaching me at some far deeper level, came again the still small voice. 'I will make you a prophet to the nations.'

I considered this statement with very mixed feelings. Half of me wanted to laugh—it sounded like such a funny idea. I had visions of sprinting round from country to country proclaiming things. Join the jet set! I can't really remember when it was, perhaps 1969 or 1970, but it was at a time when my three children were little. My days consisted of breakfast, the school run, shopping, cooking, household chores, tea, supervising homework, supper. . . it hardly left much time for sprinting to Timbuctoo with a message!

On the other hand, this sounded like the Lord speaking, and if God speaks, one dare not laugh. I considered it further. I knew this was a quote from Jeremiah. Was my mind playing tricks on me? Was I just recalling familiar scripture? But why this particular verse? I'd heard of housebound housewives who had fantasies of being film stars. Perhaps this was just a fantasy. Perhaps, rather than producing film star fantasies my subconscious had dredged up the idea that it would be glamorous to be a prophet.

But the message I had heard triggered off other thoughts. A few years previously, in 1966, I'd had a very traumatic day. All day long I'd sensed that a national disaster was impending and would take place the next day. I'd no idea what form the disaster would take. My mind went through every possibility: a nuclear explosion; an invasion; an earthquake; what? I couldn't point to any of these things, but my spirit was deeply troubled, and I paced up and down like a caged animal—waiting.

The next day the Aberfan disaster took place. A coal tip moved and fell on a school, burying alive and wiping out a whole generation of children in a Welsh mining village. The Duke of Edinburgh, representing the monarch, and the Bishop of Llandaff, for the church, went to the scene, thus confirming the accident as a national disaster.

I sat on my bed, stunned. This was what I had been waiting for: I recognised it when it happened. What should I have done? If God impresses something on a person, surely he doesn't do so for fun? Surely it is for that person to act? But act how? I hadn't even prayed; I had simply been agitated. I was terribly sad, grieving for the villagers, and feeling in my immaturity that I had let them down, and let God down. I thought of Moses, who asked God to blot him out, rather than the people in the wilderness, and of St Paul who said he could wish himself cut off from Christ for the sake of his fellow Jews. I had not prayed these things: I had simply not prayed, full stop. What should I have done?

While still wondering, I read my appointed scripture for the day, from the book of Amos. Chapter three, verse seven spoke straight to my heart. 'Surely the Lord God does nothing, without revealing his secret to his servants the prophets.' It was as if God said to me: I wasn't expecting you to do anything; I was merely informing you of what is happening.

This was the first inkling I'd ever had of being included amongst the prophets. I'd wondered about that verse a great deal. It was an indirect suggestion, but not a direct word. But on this occasion, as I walked along the Earls Court Road, it *was* a direct word: 'I will make you a prophet to the nations.' My mind also went back to the Central Hall, Westminster. 'Ye shall receive power, after that the Holy Ghost is come upon you, and ye shall be witnesses unto me in Jerusalem, in Judaea, in Samaria, and unto the uttermost part of the earth.' Perhaps this witnessing was going to take the form of prophesying to far-flung nations?

My husband is a very sane and sensible man. I felt that if I greeted him with the announcement that God had said that he was going to make me a prophet, Michael would be tempted to look around for the nearest strait-jacket! So finally I said to the Lord, 'Well, Lord, if that's what you want to do, I don't see why you shouldn't. You're God, after all, and you can do what you like, and it's OK by me, as long as you tell me what to say.' After all, if he didn't tell me what to say, then I needn't say anything. That would be easy. And if he wanted me to say something, he would have to tell me what to say, otherwise I shouldn't know what to say. So there was no point in fussing about it. 'Lord, I don't see how you're going to bring this about, but then it's not up to me, it's up to you. You can arrange it how you like. Meanwhile I'm not going to tell anyone about it, in case I'm suffering from *folie de grandeur* and have invented the whole thing. But please, in your own time, confirm it to me, through events or through people quite outside myself to whom I have told nothing.'

I feel really ashamed, recalling this prayer. How rude we are to God, how cavalier! How we take him for granted and order him about! How patient and long suffering he is with us. He, the King of kings and Lord of lords.

Once, some time ago, he brought to my mind the phrase, 'Jesus is among you as him that serveth.' He was teaching me to be a servant, and he gave me all sorts of boring servant things to do for a few particularly bossy people, in trying circumstances. One day I got utterly fed up. 'Lord,' I said, 'I just *hate* being a servant. I much prefer it when somebody else waits on me than when I wait on somebody else. I do it because you say so, and because you were a servant, and you want your disciples to be servants. But why? What's so special about being a servant? Couldn't you have invented something more fun for your disciples to be?'

Then he answered, something like this: 'If I came to you as King of kings and Lord of lords, you'd be frightened. And if I came to you as one in authority, many people have hangups about those in authority, and would refuse to listen. And if I came to you as your equal, many people have rivalry situations with their equals, and would refuse to listen. But nobody is threatened by a servant. A servant is someone you order about. You can send him out of the room if you like, you needn't listen to him. He does jobs for you. I am your servant because I love you and out of my love for you I make myself available as your servant, so as not to frighten you off and so that people may be won to my love. That is why I want my disciples to be servants.'

It was embarrassing. The Lord God is my servant. I'm supposed to be his servant, but I'm not. I don't even know how to be a servant. I behave more like a little tin god. One day I shall come before his throne, and find on it my Lord, whom I have spent my life pushing about and ordering around. It will be so shaming. Forgive me, Lord. Please help me to have your heart of a servant.

3

Living Cells

1974 was a very important year for Michael and me. The Conservatives had lost a General Election early that year, and we were searching our hearts and praying to know what God wanted us to do while we were in Opposition. Then came a telephone call. 'We want you to come to Washington, to stay in Fellowship House,' came Wallace Haines' familiar voice.

'Who's we?' I asked, 'And what's Fellowship House?'

'Fellowship House is where Congressmen and Senators and all sorts of Christians meet for fellowship. And "we" is Billy Graham and Doug Coe.'

As he spoke a paean of praise welled up inside me. I thought I would explode with joy. There also surfaced in my memory those words I had heard in the Central Hall. Could these be the 'kings and governors' God had spoken of twenty years before?

We spent the first week of May in Fellowship House. It was a revelation. Each day we were invited to breakfast with a different group: lawyers, Red Indians, a black group. Michael met with Congressmen and Senators, and spoke to a group in the Pentagon which included generals. I went to groups in the State Department and the Pentagon, and to a congressional wives group. In all these areas there was a network of cells, groups of Christians meeting in fellowship, sharing ideas and the scriptures, and praying together. We were twice entertained to dinner in

Fellowship House by a cross section of people belonging to different groups. Here was a living organic growth, members of the Body of Christ coming away from their individual cells and merging together in a quite different cluster. I got very excited. There was life and dynamism about these people and they were Christians involved together in their different spheres of work; not simply Christians leading compartmentalized lives—church on Sunday and secular life on weekdays.

I was reminded of a time when I'd been at prayer during my student days in Paris in 1955. It seemed at that time that I was given a glimpse of heaven. The impression I had was of a huge system of cells, like myriads of amoeba, all individuals, but, as they touched each other becoming one. Jesus was at the centre, but as these amoebae all connected and merged, then he became the whole mass. The connecting fluid that joined them all together, the sap or life blood or whatever, was love. The strength of this love engulfed me and made me weak. It was a stronger sensation than I had ever encountered before, indeed an experience *beyond* sensation. Now in Washington I was seeing some of these cells take on a visible form.

Abraham Vereide, a Norwegian immigrant to the USA earlier this century, was the founder of the work of the Fellowship. A pastor with a gift for personal work, he would walk into Congressmen's offices, talk to them about their problems, then pray with them. When he found two or three likeminded people in the same sphere of work, be they business people, lawyers, Congressmen, or whatever, he would introduce them to each other and suggest they meet together for prayer and discussion of their common concerns. Soon these little cells started springing up everywhere, meeting for prayer breakfasts. During the time of General Eisenhower's presidency, the group in the Congress and the group in the Senate decided to meet together and invite the President to breakfast. So started the first of the now annual National Prayer Breakfasts, attended by the President.

We have now had the privilege of attending three of these National Breakfasts: the first one of Jimmy Carter's Presidency, and two of Ronald Reagan's. At the last one there were nearly 4,000 people from 120 nations. These were mostly people in government, but all were people from little fellowship groups dotted around all over the globe; a network of living cells, black, brown, white, yellow, meeting together in Christ's name.

At that first visit in May of 1974, I was particularly struck by the congressional wives group, to which I was invited as a parliamentary wife. About seventy women met every two weeks in the morning for coffee, to listen to a speaker, to discuss, enjoy fellowship and pray together. I was deeply moved. Since I was eighteen I had been involved in women's bible study groups, and when Michael entered Parliament in 1964 I had longed for some such group in Parliament, where the wives of MPs of all parties could meet together to pray for the work of Parliament. But however much I tried to do something about it, nothing happened. Now I had a prototype before me. Could not such a thing be done in England? I went home and prayed and thought but still nothing happened.

In the autumn of 1975 Doug Coe passed through London on his way home from a trip to different European countries, and spent the night at our home. Doug succeeded Abraham Vereide, after the latter's death, as leader of the work in Washington, and is a man with a fine, sensitive gift of leadership. During our conversation, which went on late into the night, he made two unconnected comments that stuck in my mind: the first was that he saw me as a hostess in Fellowship work in London; the second was that George Thomas (now Lord Tonypandy), who was soon to become Speaker of the House of Commons, had told him that he would love to see the Speaker's House used in some way for Christian work and fellowship.

It was during 1977 that the project finally took root. In February that year Michael and I were again in Washington, this time for Jimmy Carter's first Prayer Breakfast. I was again invited to the congressional wives group, this time as the speaker. And it was now that my longing focussed into practical possibility.

On our return to London I went to see the wife of another MP, with whom I had been involved in bible study in a friend's house. We decided to invite such friends as we thought might be interested from amongst the parliamentary wives to see what might be done, so we sent out postcards and a little group of six of us met all that summer to pray and talk together. From that came the decision to hold a tea party in November that year, and invite a much larger group of parliamenary wives to share with them the idea of forming a group to pray together for the work of

Parliament. The question was where to meet? Then I remembered Doug Coe's comment about the Speaker, and we determined to ask him if we might meet in the Speaker's House.

From that time the group has grown. The Parliamentary Wives Christian Group has met every Tuesday while Parliament sits, for discussion, bible study, prayer and fellowship, since January 1978. Every term we give a dinner with a guest speaker talking about some aspect of Christian life, and to which about eighty people come, men and women from the Houses of Lords and Commons, members of all political parties and all denominations. The wives cook the meal and bring the food. All this takes place in the Speaker's House with Mr Speaker as host.

During the early days of this development, I belonged to another little prayer group. As we prayed we had a picture of the corridors of power, dark and gloomy, and as we prayed it was as if we were opening windows to let the Holy Spirit in to sweep out the gloom with his light. We also had the impression of Jesus saying that he would love to move through the Houses of Parliament, but that he needed us to help him.

'How come you need our help Lord?' we asked. 'Aren't you God? Can't you do what you like?' The answer came that he didn't want to come in wrath and judgement, but that he wanted to come in love. For that he needed his bride, his body, to co-operate with him and show forth his love.

The first three years were very hard going. Each Tuesday a blackness came over me. I struggled with depression and oppression. Once, in our intercession group, I cried out to the Lord and asked him why I so dreaded Tuesdays. I wanted to serve him, but with gladness, not with dread. The answer came that it wasn't much fun for him either in Gethsemane. He endured the cross for the joy that was set before him. It felt as though a great ploughing and churning up of rocky soil was going on through my soul. Then in October of 1981 this changed. I suddenly realized the whole thing felt quite different, as if I were sitting back and watching little seedlings sprout out of the earth. October 1982 felt different again. By this time they had developed into a sturdy little shrub, with growth and vitality and unity.

Since Christmas 1981 the leadership of this group has passed into the very capable hands of Susie Stanley, and I am able to sit back and be refreshed by the growth of love in the body of Christ in Parliament. Cells are forming and organic growth is taking root, so that we might try to affect the thinking and atmosphere of Parliament, in order that God may be recognised as Sovereign.

It was most exciting in February this year to hear the reports of several of our group who had returned from the National Prayer Breakfast in Washington, having experienced for themselves the excitement of these living cells in government throughout the world.

4

A new vision

When I was a child I was very religious, and from the age of ten prayed hard that God would show me what he wanted me to do with my life. When I was seventeen and in my last term at school and still having no idea about my future, I picked up a magazine one day and read an article about crime and prisons in America. I put down the article aware suddenly that this was the work God wanted me to do.

I was really appalled. My father was a diplomat and I had spent my life in foreign capitals, always in embassy circles. I knew nothing whatever of crime and the seamier side of life. I was in turmoil for several days, then after a particularly restless day I knelt to say the Lord's Prayer. At 'Thy will be done' I hesitated, because I knew that saying that meant committing myself to work in prisons, and I was so afraid. Finally I said it, and committed myself, then great peace settled on me and I slept. Two days later I had a letter from a friend who was a novice in a convent. She had asked the nuns to pray for me and that particularly restless day they had offered prayers for me in their chapel services, that I should know what God had for me to do.

The following spring, March 1954, a friend of mine took me to hear Billy Graham at Harringay. I was amazed at the joy of his team; they were 'serving the Lord with gladness', whereas I was wanting to serve him, but with fear and stress. Two verses Billy quoted struck me; one was, 'I am the way, the truth and the life; no man can come to the Father but by me.' I had never seen the point of Jesus before—it was always God I wanted to please. Now I saw that he was the way to God. And the second verse was, 'Casting all your care upon him, for he careth for you.' I was so relieved that somebody was prepared to take the strain, because I was feeling so stressed. So I went forward at the end of the meeting and asked Christ into my life. And from that time forward the whole emphasis of my commitment changed. It was now no longer that I had to go to prisons and borstals, but rather that Jesus, out of his love for people, wanted to go into the prisons, and he was merely inviting me to go along with him. So the whole thing became an adventure.

I next trained to do social work at the London School of Economics, and then worked in a Salvation Army approved school for 15-18-year-old girls (a VD treatment school), and then at what is now called the Henderson Hospital. At that time it was a social rehabilitation unit for psychopaths run by Dr Maxwell Jones. I was a social therapist, attached to a men's ward of twenty-eight men aged from eighteen to sixty.

I learnt many spiritual lessons there, and among them a very important one that changed my attitude to people greatly. Up until this time I had no conviction of sin. I knew generally that I was a sinner—at least I didn't dare contradict that view—but I had no sense of my own sinfulness, having been a 'goody-goody' all my life, trying hard to obey the law. At the unit the treatment was group therapy, and what happened to me was that time after time while some man or woman in the group was under the spotlight in discussion, the Holy Spirit would shine into the recesses of my heart and show me something in myself similar to the person under discussion. It wasn't long before I realised that there wasn't anything wrong in anyone else that wasn't wrong in me too. It was a most painful experience; I was ill twice and lost a great deal of weight as I became aware of the awfulness of sin, and of my own sinfulness. It changed my attitude, because if you are not conscious of your own sin, you are as I was, like the Pharisee in Luke 18, and you become self-righteous and hard towards sinners. But when you realise what Jesus saved you from, then you are filled with love for others and long to share with them God's forgiveness and love. Jesus said of Mary Magdalene that her love was so great because she had been forgiven so much. The experience also gave me a tiny glimpse of what it was like for Jesus to 'be made sin for us, who knew no sin' (2 Cor. 5:21).

In 1958 Michael and I got married and for eighteen years nothing that happened in my life had any connection with the work I had hoped to do in prisons. I often longed to go into a prison, but I couldn't think how to get there, or what I would do if I did get there. So I stayed at home and looked after our three children, wondering what all the training had been for.

Then, in that first visit to Fellowship House in Washington, Michael met Chuck Colson. He had been Special Counsel to President Nixon, had recently become a Christian, and was at that time awaiting trial for offences connected with Watergate. His story is vividly told in his book *Born Again*. Michael met him on a visit to Boston, where they were guests of Tom Phillips, the man through whom Chuck had become a Christian, and they struck up a friendship. Michael wrote to him in prison and, in the summer of 1976, Doug Coe telephoned and asked us if we would have Chuck and his wife and daughter to stay with us in London for two weeks during their European trip. We were delighted to have them, and from then a new adventure started.

While Chuck was staying with us that summer he told us about his plans. He had started a little prayer and Bible discussion fellowship with other prisoners while he was himself in prison, and though he had not yet committed himself to what has since become Prison Fellowship in America, he had started schemes for training and discipling prisoners for Christ. As he spoke my heart started to stir, and all my preparation of twenty years previously came to my mind. However, I said nothing.

The following January, the time of Jimmy Carter's first Prayer Breakfast, we stayed with the Colsons in Washington, and were in Chuck's office on the day when the Federal Head of Prisons gave Chuck permission to go into forty prisons for teaching and training. I shared with the office staff a prophecy that Jean Darnall had brought to us, that God was going to bring revival to the prisons throughout the world and that this was going to be through prisoners sharing Christ with each other.

March 1978 found me travelling in the States with Jean Darnall, and Chuck arranged for me to visit Pleasanton, a women's prison near San Francisco, on the same day as a Prison Fellowship team was going in to conduct a seminar. A few days before this the Lord impressed on me that I would be speaking to these women and he gave me the verse about Jesus from Psalm 22, 'I am a worm, and no man' to talk about. I was very surprised as I hadn't expected to be speaking to them. At a prayer meeting a couple of days before the visit, someone had a picture of these women's hearts, very hard, with iron bars across them. As I spoke these words the bars would open and the women's hearts would be set free. So I was very excited about that. The whole visit—my first time ever in a prison-was an amazing experience for me. I felt so at home there, totally identified with the prisoners and also at one with the visiting team. I felt that I could have spent the rest of my life there. When I was asked to speak, and spoke out the words Jesus gave me, I knew I had perfect communication with the women. And at the end of the evening several of them came to shake my hand, and their faces were shining.

I returned to England bemused, and in April that year Michael and I went to a Christian conference with Lord Longford. When I was eighteen someone had suggested that if I wanted to work for prisoners I should ring up Lord Longford and ask if I could work for him. However I was much too shy to do any such thing. On this occasion, the first time I had ever met him, we just chatted about Chuck's work in America. But after breakfast the next day he came to me and said: 'I have very strong guidance, and my guidance is that you are going to initiate Prison Fellowship in England.' He didn't know anything about me, or my past experience, at all. He went on: 'I thought I was going to do something about it, but God said "No, you are to stand back. Mrs Alison is going to do it." ' I was stunned, but equally I recognised the authority of what he said. At last everything was fitting into place.

'Well,' said Lord Longford, 'you're leader. So what shall we do?' Dazed, the only thing I could think of was that verse where Jesus says, 'Where two or three are gathered together in my name there am I in the midst.' I suggested that we might collect two or three people and pray together, and ask Jesus what he would like to do with us. 'Right,' said Lord Longford. 'Whom shall we have?'

Our first meeting, later in April, consisted of Lord Longford, Michael, Anthony Cordle and me, and took place in an interview room in the House of Lords. We prayed and worshipped together, and agreed to meet again, and next time Anthony invited John Harris and Ross Simpson to join us. Fortnightly throughout the summer of 1978 we met and prayed, and from this emerged a desire to have a conference to which we would invite as many Christians from all over England, and from all denominations, who were already involved with prisons, that we could find, and we would invite Chuck Colson to share with us how Prison Fellowship started in America and what God was doing through that.

5

A child is born

During that summer, leading up to the '78 November Conference, I received a letter from Chuck Colson saying that he would come and speak to us, but also assuming that we were doing a number of things, none of which we were doing. When I received this letter I caved in, in a feeling of total inadequacy and uselessness. 'What are we supposed to be doing, Lord?' I asked. 'I don't know the first thing about prisons. I haven't the faintest idea what we are supposed to do. In fact we're not doing anything; we're just sitting in a heap, praying. I'm supposed to be leader of this thing and I haven't the least idea where I am leading anybody to.'

Armed with this complaint, I went to our intercession group and wailed at the Lord, 'Lord, help! *What* are we supposed to be *doing*?'

As we prayed, the Lord gave us a picture of a house. It was a very big house and took in the whole of England. Because it was so big the foundations had to be very deep. The ground floor of this house was the prison population and the people that the rest of society have cast off, and then the other floors were all the different sectors of society: at the very top, as a covering to this house, was the Throne and the Crown. The Lord impressed on us that he was shaking up the whole of society, and that we were not to be worried by this shaking; he was rebuilding, from the foundations upward, according to his holiness and righteousness. As we waited on him further he impressed on us the verse from Psalm: 127 'Except the Lord build the house, they labour in vain that build it'. And then, as an added bonus, the further verse from the same Psalm: 'He giveth to his beloved in sleep'. It was as if he were saying, 'Don't worry about it, I'm building this house. You can relax.'

It was amazing. What new adventure was the Lord leading us into? What a breathtaking revelation! As I searched the Scriptures that summer I was drawn to Exodus 35, where Moses calls the people together to build a tabernacle. He calls to the people of willing and generous hearts, to give of their gifts and skills to help build the tabernacle. As I prayed about it, it seemed that we were to call together men and women of generous hearts, Christians of all denominations already involved in the prisons: probation officers, social workers, prison staff, visitors, magistrates, police, solicitors, ex-prisoners, intercessors, businessmen, housewives and share with them what God was doing, and then they would offer their gifts and skills to help build the house. The Lord also impressed on me that he wanted all the prison chaplains involved, because he was collecting his whole body, from all denominations, and the chaplains are the pastors of the flock. With this in mind, I asked the Chaplain General of Prisons if I might come and see him and talk to him about it.

Early in July 1978 there was a Service of Thanksgiving in Westminster Abbey for 100 years of the Prison Service. Michael and I were invited, as at that time Michael was an Opposition front-bench spokesman on Home Affairs. All the chaplains, led by the Chaplain General, processed up the aisle. The address was given by the Catholic Bishop of Middlesborough. I sat there thinking of the things that God had said that he was going to do. As the prisons crumbled, he was going to set up a network of living stones to take care of the prison population.

For many years I have had the habit of reading the verse of Scripture in *The Times* each day, and praying about it. Often the Lord has drawn my attention to something through it. The day of the Thanksgiving Service at the Abbey happened to be my birthday, so a few days previously I had asked the Lord if he would very kindly give me a verse in *The Times*, to encourage me, or direct me, as a birthday present. Up till that time I had kept God's word in my heart, or had perhaps shared it with a few like-minded friends, but I had not spoken it out in public. Now the time was coming when I was going to have to speak out what God was going to do. I had an appointment to see the Chaplain General a few days later, and we were also to hold a meeting in a committee room in the House of Lords in July, to which we had invited seventy people. I was extremely nervous.

That morning found me in a state of great anticipation, running to the front door for the papers, and my birthday verse. It was Luke 1:45 : 'Blessed is she that believed: for there shall be a performance of those things which were told her from the Lord.'

God's ways are not our ways.

At the November Conference in Church House, Westminster, 170 people were present. We had a most exciting presentation from Chuck Colson and his aide, Gordon Loux, of the work of Prison Fellowship in America. They put forward all sorts of ideas. The most important of these was the concept of taking a teacher and team of Christians into the prison to hold a week's seminar. Another aspect of their work was to bring out twelve prisoners, two from each of six different prisons, for a two week training and discipling conference. Then they are sent back to finish their time in prison, but as Christian cell leaders, to share their faith with other prisoners.

The shape the conference should take had been very clear to me, all except the last hour. Who should sum up at the end? What should be done at that time? As I prayed it was impressed on me that I should stand there, and that God would bring forth a baby. Just that. I don't know what I was going to say, or what anyone else would say. Just that God was going to bring forth a baby.

It was a most painful last hour. I hadn't dared tell the men about this baby so they hadn't the faintest idea what I was going to do. I didn't know myself. We had started well, but as I stood there all sorts of anger and hostility and negative reactions came from all over the floor. There were some people there who had worked in prisons for many years and thought that nothing new could or should be done. The high level of expectancy sank to rock bottom. Everything seemed to disintegrate. I finally sat down and handed the meeting to Michael. He salvaged the situation by calling for a further conference in March 1979.

That weekend was terrible. How could I have been so nutty as to think that I could stand on a platform, and a baby would be born? Was it just pride that had made me take that last hour? Should I have asked one of the men to preside over it? Was I merely trying to assert myself as leader over them? I was very sad. I had clearly let God down. I had misunderstood him, or misheard him. Anyhow, a baby hadn't been born.

On Monday afternoon I weighed myself and found that I had lost seven pounds in weight since Friday evening. I then collapsed with exhaustion and depression and sadness.

On Tuesday I received a lovely letter from Tony Ralls, an ex-prisoner who had been at the conference. 'God wants to encourage you,' he wrote, 'because you have just given birth to a spiritual baby, and you are suffering from post-natal depression. And it doesn't matter about being weak and foolish, because God uses weak things and foolish things.'

God's ways are not our ways.

In March I was able to share this with the second conference that Michael had convened. This little baby would grow up and develop to adulthood as all of us, of all denominations, of all sectors of society with different gifts and skills and roles and functions, brothers and sisters in Christ, met together and worshipped and prayed for the prisons and prisoners and looked to see what God would have us do. There would be little cells, twos and threes gathered together in Christ's name, little nuclei to which more people could attach themselves, a group in the end for each of the 123 prisons in the country, a core group to take on the responsibility of being the centre of a far larger group. The vision was of cells, birth, a baby, organic growth – as we see in nature; God's ways, not man's structures. The Incarnation, Emmanuel, God with us.

So with the unanimity of the entire group, Prison Christian Fellowship was launched.

6

'. . . in Jerusalem and in Judaea. . .'

One of the people who came to that first conference at Church House was Rev. David Jardine, who had a ministry to prisoners in Crumlin Road Prison, Belfast. He told me about some of the wonderful things God was doing amongst the prisoners: men coming to Christ and meeting for fellowship and bible study; growing as Christians in their little groups; conversions amongst the terrorists both loyalist and republican. The difficulty was when they left prison and went back to their ghettoes: how were they to stand as Christians when they were being urged on to further violence, and punished for failing to obey orders?

My heart went out to this man. I longed to go and be with him in Crumlin Road Prison. However I didn't see how this was to come about.

The following spring, April 1979, there was a general election. Mrs Thatcher became Prime Minister, and in May she appointed Michael as Minister of State for Northern Ireland with, amongst other things, responsibility for the prisons. I had to laugh. God certainly gives one the desires of one's heart!

I felt as if I were on a mission for the King of kings. Each time we flew over in the RAF plane, and stayed in Stormont House or Hillsborough Castle, I prayed that someone would cross my path, someone who would be relevant for Prison Fellowship, Protestant or Catholic. I longed to go into a prison, but Michael wouldn't allow me to until we really understood the situation there. He was also Minister responsible for Health in Northern Ireland, so he said that what would help him was if I went round the mental hospitals and psychiatric units, as I had had relevant experience, as a social worker. I was half reluctant to do this, but felt that if I did my stuff in the mental hospitals, I might be allowed into the prisons as a reward for good behaviour!

But all the time my understanding was being enlarged. God had said that the ground floor of the house he had shown me was the prison population and the people that the rest of society had cast off. I hadn't really taken in who these other people might be. But now as I went round the mental hospitals, it was as if the Holy Spirit was nudging me and saying, 'Look. . . these people are part of my ground floor too.'

Eventually, in February 1980, we went to a service in the chapel of Crumlin Road Prison, with David Jardine preaching. It was a beautiful service. Terrorists who had come to faith in Christ played guitars and sang their testimonies. I was thrilled to be there. It was a communion service and I very much wanted to take communion with the prisoners, but the Governor told us we must leave the chapel before the communion. I was so distressed. I asked Michael if he could go out with the Governor and the detectives, and if I could stay and take communion with the prisoners. Michael said no, we must do as we were told and not make any fuss.

I tore myself away from the chapel with a terrible pain in my heart. I so wanted to stay. When I got home the intensity of that pain was so great that I could do nothing but lie on my bed and weep. 'What's the matter with me Lord?' I said. 'Why have I got this pain?'

Then God explained it to me, through the verse in Romans 5: '. . . the love of God is shed abroad in our hearts by the Holy Spirit which is given to us'. What he gave me to understand was that he wanted to pour out his love through the prisons, through the very heart of the terrorist situation, in such strength that it would sweep out before it all the fear and intimidation and hatred. But in order to do this, he needed a body through which to express this love. If you love somebody and if you are unable to express this love for some reason, your whole body aches. This was the pain I was feeling, Jesus' pain. This body that he needed had to be not one person, or two or three people, but the whole body of Christ, Catholic and Protestant together, loving one another, sharing fellowship together, a united body through which he could pour his love, the 'perfect love which casts out fear'.

William Fitch, a Belfast accountant and well-known in evangelical circles, had invited Chuck Colston to Belfast to speak at a special showing of his film *Born Again*. I asked William if I could possibly borrow a morning out of Chuck's busy schedule, to hold a very private meeting, to which we would invite the forty-five people on my list of Christians involved in prison work in Northern Ireland. William agreed to this, and we held a meeting, to which twenty-seven people came, and Chuck and Gordon Loux talked about

Prison Fellowship, and shared this concept of God's love being poured out through one body. Unanimously the people there wanted to start this work in Northern Ireland.

We had one further meeting at which Ross Simpson and I shared with them the concept of a few people of all denominations forming a core group to take on the responsibility for Northern Ireland, and then it was over to them. They set up their own group, their own charitable trust, and appointed a Catholic and a Protestant as co-workers, to go into the prisons together. Now, after two years of praying, in one prison the prisoners of both denominations are coming together in fellowship, crossing the divide. In the other prisons it hasn't happened yet. Protestants are coming to Christ in Protestant groups and Catholics in Catholic groups, but there is still a great divide between them. They need our prayers, that the love of God might draw them together and break down the barriers.

When we held our first conference at Church House, visitors from Scotland had come, asking Chuck Colson to visit Scotland to talk to them about Prison Fellowship. From that time we prayed about how to proceed in Scotland.

By early 1980 we had made a policy decision not to try to run Prison Fellowship in Northern Ireland or in Scotland from London, but rather to go to those countries and find core groups of committed Christians, already involved in the prison service, to take on the responsibility for those countries. In each place the prison administration was different, the network of relationships was different. In order for a movement of the Holy Spirit to change a society, Christian people, in whom dwells God's Spirit, need to be in strategic places within those structures.

In Northern Ireland the opportunity came almost immediately after Prison Fellowship in England and Wales was launched. What about Scotland?

In May 1978 I had been invited to Glasgow to speak at a dinner to launch the Lydia Fellowship in Scotland.

The Lydia Fellowship was started by Shelagh McAlpine. She and Joy Dawson had met to pray and intercede in New Zealand for several years, and when the McAlpines came to England, Shelagh collected together two or three women in Sussex to start praying for this country. This little group grew and multiplied, and soon little groups started springing up all over the country. They called themselves Lydia from the seller of purple in the book of Acts, who was converted through Paul's preaching and opened her home to the Christians.

Then news of a remarkable prophecy reached Shelagh, and greatly encouraged her and all the Lydia movement. In Jerusalem there lived a nun called Mother Barbara. She was a Romanoff, of the Tsar's family, and in 1911 she had gone to a monastery in Russia to ask the monks to pray for her family who were in danger from the revolutionaries. One of the monks had a prophecy, and his prophecy included many things. One was that Russia would flow with rivers of blood, one that Germany would be cut in two, and one was that Britain would come to the brink of destruction, but would be saved by praying women.

I first met this group when Jeanne Harper, until recently their leader, invited me to speak at their annual conference in 1977, to share about items in Parliament that needed prayer. I asked them to pray for the formation of the group in Parliament, which took place that year. The Lydia Fellowship has grown and grown. It was with a Lydia group in Canterbury the following April that we first shared our dreams of a Prison Fellowship. And they gave us our first cheque as seed money for the Fellowship. It was to the Lydias that I wrote when we envisaged a conference in in Church House with Chuck as speaker, and they who sent us the names of Christians involved in prisons throughout the country. And whenever we have a prayer request I ring them up and they send our requests throughout their prayer chains.

So it was to the Lydias in Scotland that I wrote asking for names of Christians involved in prisons, and we started a list of people in Scotland as we had in Northern Ireland.

In December 1980 I received an invitation from Louise Purvis, the wife of John Purvis, a Member of the European Parliament, to come to Scotland the following June to speak about the Parliamentary Wives Group to a Christian women's luncheon club, and also to speak to a Lydia Fellowship prayer group. I felt this was an important invitation that I must accept. All the time we were feeling for an opening for Prison Fellowship. How would this come about? Surely speaking to a group of women wouldn't start

Prison Fellowship in Scotland? Still I might meet some relevant person. I accepted the invitation although June '81 was an impossible time for me. We were due to move house that month.

In April '81 Louise telephoned me to make final arrangements. She had read Chuck Colson's *Born Again*, she said, if there was anything she could do to help Prison Fellowship take off in Scotland, she'd be delighted.

Then the idea struck me. Would she like to ask the people on our list to a meeting? Then I could share with them the vision of Prison Fellowship and they could decide for themselves if they wanted to start it, and invite Chuck Colson to speak to them. She quickly agreed. We had only six weeks. She invited them all to lunch in her home near St Andrews and twenty of the thirty or so people accepted, and travelled from all over Scotland to come to the lunch.

It was a most exciting though stressful week. We moved house on the Monday, and on Tuesday I flew to Edinburgh, to be met by Louise and her comforting hospitality. We had a marvellous lunch meeting on Wednesday with most dedicated men and women, already involved in the prison scene. And at that meeting was the core group that came together to take on the responsibility for Prison Fellowship Scotland. Louise agreed to hers being the address to whom people wrote so that there should be one centre for communications, to avoid confusion.

Later that year William Fitch of Northern Ireland was asked to arrange Chuck's visit which took place in November '81, and then Prison Fellowship Scotland was officially launched.

'You shall be witnesses unto me, both in Jerusalem and in Judaea, then in Sumaria, and unto the uttermost parts of the earth.'

7
'. . . to the uttermost parts of the earth'

In October 1979 Michael and I had a lovely holiday in Canada and New England. We'd gone to stay with friends in Boston, then flew to Canada for a few days before driving slowly back to Boston enjoying the beautiful scenery and changing colours of the New England fall.

We had arrived utterly exhausted. Prison Fellowship England and Wales had been launched in March that year, then in April there had been the General Election. In May Michael was appointed Minister of State in Northern Ireland, and we spent the rest of that summer bouncing back and forth between London and Belfast, like yo-yos. By the autumn we were very weary and flew out to stay with friends and relax.

One Sunday morning we were sitting in church in Toronto, when suddenly it seemed as though the Holy Spirit was starting to impress on me how to set up Prison Fellowship in Canada. My heart sank.

I thought Our Lord was asking us to do this while we were there, only another three days! I shrank from the idea of any more work. However the impression grew stronger and clearer, and after a while I became aware that God was also impressing on me how to set up Prison Fellowship in Australia. At this point I became intrigued. Surely he couldn't expect me to do something in Australia while I was in Canada. Perhaps I had better just listen and stop fussing.

Then someone stood up and read the lesson: it was 2 Samuel 7, where David says he would like to build a temple for the Lord. This passage of Scripture broke in on my thoughts; I felt it had something to do with this revelation about Canada and Australia, but I couldn't imagine what.

When Michael and I were together I shared this with him. 'What can this passage mean?' I said. 'What's it got to do with Canada and Australia?'

We read it and Michael pointed out that King David wanted to build a temple for God, but the Lord, speaking through the prophet Nathan, said: not at all, it wasn't David who was going to build a house for God, but God who was going to build a house for David and for his seed, and for ever.

As we read and discussed, another picture filled my mind. This time it was like seeing two photographs, one superimposed on the other. The first 'photograph' was a map of the world, a very interesting and unusual looking map– and although I was most conscious of Canada and Australia, all the countries were there. The second, superimposed, picture was a map of the Kingdom of Heaven. This was triangular in shape: Jesus was the top angle, but somehow he was all of it as well. It was a three-dimensional picture going back and forth in time. People like St Francis of Assisi were there, milling about. It was made up of people, who were taken from every nation of the earth, and it was a body; all the people joining up became different parts of it.

Then the picture shifted and became a building, made up of living stones. Suddenly I realized that the ground floor of this building was the prison population, and the people that the rest of society have cast off; then the different floors were the different sectors of society, ending up with the roof of this building, which was the King of kings, and Lord of lords, seated on his throne. I realized that this was the same house that I had seen in England, only this time I was seeing it world-wide. It was also the same house that God had said he was going to build for King David, and for his seed forever, and for which the tabernacle, and the temple in the Old Testament were visual aids.

For the next couple of days I felt weak and dazed. I also wondered what I should do with this information about Canada and Australia. Finally I thought, perhaps I should ring Chuck Colson and tell him. Maybe it's his business rather than mine. So on Tuesday evening I rang Chuck, very nervously, at his home in Washington. I thought that he would think I'd flipped! When I got through to him I said: 'In church on Sunday God showed me how to set up Prison Fellowship in Canada and in Australia.' There was a pause, then Chuck said: 'Do you know what I've been doing today?'

'No'

'I've been in a meeting and we've been trying to work out how to set up Prison Fellowship in Canada and in Australia.'

How wonderful is God! How mighty are his works!

The following year, September 1980, Chuck called together his first Prison Fellowship International Board meeting. It was amazing to think that five years previously Chuck had been in prison himself, and now Prison Fellowship had been launched in USA, England, Northern Ireland, Canada, Australia and

New Zealand. And people from sixty-four other countries had written to Washington to make enquiries about setting it up in their countries.

. . . The ground floor of God's house, worldwide. . .

The next time I went to a Board meeting in Washington, the following February, another thing struck me forcefully. I was stunned to see a beautiful map of the world on the wall, in a very fine glass case. What struck me was not so much that it was beautiful and unusually decorated, but that it was the same map that I had seen in the visual image I'd had in Canada. Could I be imagining things, I wondered? I went round the office and looked at a couple of atlases. Perhaps all maps of the world look the same, I thought. But no. The atlas maps were clearly not what I had seen. The map on the wall was.

After the Board meeting I asked Kathryn Grant, the Board's secretary, how the map had got there. She said nobody really knew. Someone had given it to them as a present. Somebody else had appeared, with a skill for glass framing, and had made a frame and put it up. Nobody had authorized it. Suddenly there it was. On this map are little flags to show in what countries Prison Fellowship is forming. It was a breathtaking experience.

In September 1981 Michael and I went abroad again, this time to Australia and New Zealand. Two years previously we'd had a visit in London from the Rev. James Worsfold of New Zealand. We discussed Prison Fellowship and he asked us if we would go to New Zealand and share with his colleagues what we were doing in England. I sensed a quickening of the spirit as he spoke. The verse came back to me, '. . . witnesses unto me. . . in Judea, Samaria and unto the uttermost part of the earth'. Surely New Zealand was the uttermost part of the earth from us in England? But how could we possibly envisage making the expensive trip to New Zealand?

The following year again James Worsfold came to England. Again he asked us to come. Again my spirit leaped. So I began to pray in earnest. Later that year Michael decided that we should go out to Australia on business, and should take our next year's annual leave to go. And then, at the February 1981 Prison Fellowship International Board meeting, Chuck asked Peter Blaxall of New Zealand and me to come to the next year's Board meeting with suggestions for our first Triennial Symposium, bringing together people from many countries to pray and think together about those in prison. That clinched it. When we went to Australia that September we would also go to New Zealand to talk to Peter.

Our three day visit to New Zealand was wonderful. We arrived in Wellington and attended the Governor's Prayer Breakfast. We were met by Peter Blaxall and entertained by the people who had set up the Prayer Breakfast, who were also the trustees of Prison Fellowship New Zealand. These were a group of people who had attended the Washington Prayer Breakfast in 1978 and had started the movement in New Zealand. Part of the living cells of the body, world-wide.

That evening, as the British High Commissioner was ill, the Assistant High Commissioner gave a reception for us, as Michael although on a holiday visit, was a Minister in the British Government. To it came several of our new-made friends. Michael had been asked particularly to speak to the Ministry of Justice about Prison Fellowship as he was Minister responsible for prisons in Northern Ireland, and therefore knowledgable. So we were asked at this reception about Prison Fellowship in England and the value of it to those in prison. Michael spoke extremely well, and then he said, 'But my wife started it in England, and is our chairman, so she should say something about it.' So as I know very little about prisons, I just told them about this house that God is building. I could see the expression on people's faces: they looked very surprised, and very polite. But the acting High Commissioner was wonderful: as he thanked us for our talk, he slammed his fist down on the table and said: 'Isn't it *marvellous*! God is building a house!' And everybody laughed!

The next day we flew to Christchurch. The Mayor of Christchurch, also on the Advisory Council of Prison Fellowship, took us round Paparua Prison, where we met inmates looking forward to the next Saturdays' visit from the local Prison Fellowship. That evening he gave a reception for us in his mayor's parlour where we met all the local Prison Fellowship group. Again we were asked to speak.

Earlier that afternoon I had had two hours of deep depression and blackness. I longed to say sensible things about prisons. I envied Michael who, when he speaks, does say sensible things. All I could talk about was this house God is building. In the end I decided that it was no use my trying to say sensible things – if God had wanted somebody sensible he would have picked someone else! So when it came to my turn to speak I again talked about God's house. At the end of the talk a prison officer, sitting next to me, called me over. He was close to tears. Two or three weeks before, as he had been reading the Scriptures in 1 Chronicles, he felt the Holy Spirit impress on him that he was to collect together the vessels to help Solomon build the temple. Only he had no idea what this meant. He and his wife, who was sitting beside him, had prayed together, and had asked the Lord to explain to them what he wanted them to do, as they didn't understand. Now suddenly I appeared from the other end of the world, to explain this picture. Now suddenly he understood what he was supposed to be doing.

We were both in awe, but both encouraged. It is like a jigsaw puzzle, each one of us has his or her own little part to play: if we are obedient to our little bit, the sum of the bits makes up the whole picture. Only God can see the picture on the lid. What a picture! What a house!

8

'Till we have built Jerusalem'

My husband has been a Conservative Member of Parliament since 1964, first for Barkston Ash in North Yorkshire until 1983, when the boundaries were changed, and Barkston Ash ceased to exist; and in 1983 he was elected as Member for Selby, which was part of our old division, and includes several new areas. So for the last twenty years politics has been very much the stuff of our lives. And we have lived in both Yorkshire and London.

May 1979 brought in a new Conservative Government with Mrs Thatcher as Prime Minister, and as I prayed about what subject to talk about at the Lydia Annual Conference that month, the following thoughts came to mind.

In March 1966 we had a General Election. Harold Wilson had become Labour Prime Minister in October 1964 after 13 years of Tory rule, and now after eighteen months he was seeking re-election as he had a very small majority in the House of Commons. One day as I was driving the car in Yorkshire during the election campaign, again the Holy Spirit impressed words on my mind.

'I am bringing judgement on this nation through the Labour Party. Then there will come a period of blessing through the Conservatives.'

I drove on amazed. First I was flabbergasted that the Lord should bother to tell me what he was doing, and secondly, I simply didn't understand it. I am not a very politically minded person, and had I not been married to a politician would probably not take very much interest in politics. I certainly did not think God was a Conservative. Nor Labour. God is God, and political parties are human institutions, and subject to corruption and decay. Also I knew that there were Christians in the House of Commons in both parties. What could this mean?

It was no surprise, therefore when Labour won the 1966 election. I told Michael what the Holy Spirit had showed me, and one or two close friends, but mostly I kept it to myself. And I watched to see what would happen, and sought understanding.

As the 1960s went by, the nature of the Labour party changed. At the beginning there were lots of Labour Christians, people such as Methodist Ministers, but gradually as time went by they were replaced by an influx of humanists and atheists. By the end of the '60s there was a quite different Labour party. I didn't understand, and I continued to watch and pray, when two things happened in 1978 which began to give me understanding of what God had said in 1966.

One of these things was the visit to this country of President Ceaucescu of Romania. He came over on a State visit, and during his few days in England, was invited to a reception in the Speaker's House. Michael and I were also invited, and as we stood there, the Speaker, George Thomas, brought Mr Ceaucescu and his party round and introduced him to us. I was very amazed by that little encounter and handshake. The thing that struck both Michael and me was that he was grey: he looked grey, his face was grey, his eyes were dead, and he didn't look us in the eye, he looked over our shoulders as he shook hands with us. The sensation was of shaking hands with a block of wood, and the thought that struck us was that this was the opposite of abundant life, it was abundant death.

At that same reception I spoke to various other people who had been trying to entertain Mr Ceaucescu and his party: the Queen had given a reception at the Palace; a banquet had been given at the Guildhall for them. The people I spoke to said it was the mot difficult thing in the world to talk to these guests; they were wooden and unresponsive. They had tried hard to make them feel happy and at home, no one discussed politics, but still not a flicker. One man told me he had sat next to a woman at the Guildhall who spoke a certain amount of English. If he said anything quite ordinary like, 'this is nice cabbage', she would immediately respond by saying, 'we have beautiful cabbage in the People's Socialist Republic of Romania'. It was like pressing a button. You got the same response to everything. Why? Why this response as of dead people?

Later that summer someone sent me a booklet that suddenly made my thinking fall into place. It was by Richard Wurmbrand called 'Was Karl Marx a Satanist?' (available from Christian Mission to the Communist World, PO Box 19, Bromley, BR1 1DJ England.) It seems pretty clear, from the letters and writings that he quotes, that indeed Marx may have been one and therefore it is not surprising that Marxism, which has spread to and overtaken so many parts of the world, should desire to eradicate the worship of and belief in God. The whole practice of communism is a counterfeit, a lie from the Father of lies; – the brotherhood of man but without a father – a counterfeit of the Christian family relationship. God is our Father, who sent Christ, his only son to die for us, so that we might be born again into his family through receiving Christ, called in Scripture the first among many bretheren. The concept of equality has been bedevilled. Of course we are all equal in God's sight, but he has made each of us unique and special, made in God's image, with our different gifts and skills and contributions, and functions, as different from one another as are different flowers in a garden. God the creator has given us all a different creativity, a rich profusion, which comes to the full in our life in Christ and Christ in us – 'I have come that ye might have life, and have it more abundantly'. The counterfeit of equality has produced the lust for uniformity – same clothes, same houses, same education, sameness, the crushing of creativity. The abundant death that I sensed in Mr Ceacescu's handshake.

Before the 1979 election in Britain, people who were not necessarily Christians were saying, 'If we have a Labour government now, we are going to become like Eastern Europe'. One or two senior Labour politicians were saying, 'We need another proper spell of Labour government, so that we can have full blooded socialism in this country'.

As we prayed in our little intercession group before the general election that year, we had a sense that God was releasing us from a yoke of bondage as at the time when Moses took the children of Israel out of Egypt and into the Promised Land. That the period of blessing through the Conservatives, he mentioned in 1966, was about to come. But that it wouldn't be easy. As the time came for the children of Israel to be set free, Pharaoah made their life much more difficult. We had to pray for the Labour party, that it would be set free from Marxist dogma, and that a genuinely viable alternative form of democratic government would emerge from the broken shambles of the Labour party. And we had to pray for the Conservative party, that its leaders would have courage to push through their policies of freeing up the individual from the uniformity of state monopoly. As we prayed for Mrs Thatcher we had a picture of her as a lovely shining jewel, but that we needed to pray and intercede for her, as power corrupts and distorts, and the pressures are great, and she needed our constant prayer. It is God who is freeing us from the bondage and giving us new life, not people or parties. And he raises up one and puts down another.

When the people of Israel went into the Promised Land having been taken out of bondage, there was a lot of work for them to do, and they had to get rid of the Hittites and the Amorites and Canaanites and the Jebusites, and the false gods, and clear them up. God wanted them to obey his laws and show forth by their lives and communal living, his holiness and righteousness. They had to clear up the things that were wrong.

We are in a similar situation now. The whole question of sexual morality, marriage, abortion, paedophilia, pornography and homosexuality needs clearing up and laws made that reflect God's holiness. Witchcraft and the occult run riot. Before the Indecent Displays Bill became law we looked in a sex shop window to see what was displayed. I was appalled to see a Black Magic box displayed with a notice about how to fix spells on someone that you lust after. Since 1951 we've had no law to deal with witchcraft, and since then the occult has thrived.

One of the pictures we had as we prayed after the election was of a grey carpet of state control being rolled back over the country and under it, springing up all over the place, little small businesses, springing up like flowers. Creativity as opposed to passivity, life instead of death.

A scripture that came to my mind as I prayed about the talk to the Lydia conference that month came from the Book of Nehemiah. Nehemiah went back to Jerusalem to rebuild the walls which have been destroyed . . . From Nehemiah Chapter 4 (Good News Bible):

> The enemy mocked them, but they were not discouraged . . . 6ff. So we went on rebuilding the wall and soon it was half its full height, because the people were eager to work. . .
> . . . so they all plotted together to come and attack Jerusalem and create confusion, but we prayed to our God and kept men on guard against them day and night. . .
>
> Our enemies thought we would not see them or know what was happening until they were already upon us, killing us and putting an end to our work . . . but people came to warn us of the plans our enemies were making against us. . .
>
> I saw that the people were worried, so I said to them and to their leaders and officials, 'Don't be afraid of our enemies. Remember how great and

> terrifying the Lord is, and fight for your fellow-countrymen, your children, your wives and your homes'. Our enemies heard that we had found out what they were plotting, and they realized that God had defeated their plans. Then all of us went back to rebuilding the wall.
>
> From then on half my men worked and half stood guard, wearing coats of armour and armed with spears, shields, and bows. And our leaders gave full support to the people who were rebuilding the wall.

I see the people who are doing the construction as the politicians and business men and those engaged in public life, but the people standing on guard with the spears and shields as the intercessors, protecting the workmen as they build. This means putting on the whole armour of God, and being ready to do spiritual warfare to keep off the enemy while the land is being reconstructed.

Will you pray?

I still see God as God – not on the side of any political party, but the one who will set the country free from bondage.

9

The 'One Body' baby

As well as being involved in politics, Michael has been very involved in church matters all our married life. He was a lay reader in the Church of England in the early years of our marriage, and a member first of the old Church Assembly, then of the General Synod. Although in the early 1960s I was mostly occupied in looking after our three small children, born in 1959, 1961, and 1964, and also with the demands made by living in two places and nursing a constituency, I was through Michael, made aware of some of the bigger issues involved in the church, and I'd like to share some thoughts and lessons I learned.

In 1966 I went through some painful and difficult experiences in my heart and spirit, which I didn't understand at all at the time, but after it was all over the Holy Spirit explained to me that he had been taking me through the three temptations of Jesus, of course not in the way that Jesus went through them but in a way that made sense to me in my life.

The last of these experiences was very painful. The suggestion made to me was, 'All right, if you want to follow Christ that is fine, but you will come to a nasty sticky end like he did.' At that time I was about to give my testimony at a Billy Graham Crusade in Earls Court Arena that June. I was shortly to be thirty years old. At the Crusade I would be publicly proclaiming my allegiance to Christ. The temptation was to think that when Christ was thirty, he had only three years to live. And the suggestion was that I would be killed through Satanists and black magic people.

For three days and three nights I was really terrified. I would wake in the night pouring sweat – '. . . the terror by night'. During the day I would find it difficult to walk down the passage: my joints felt like water, my bones didn't seem to fit into each other. In the middle of this panic the verse from 2 Timothy 1 came into my mind: 'God has not given us a spirit of fear, but of power and of love and of a sound mind.' I stopped dead in my tracks and thought, there is something funny about all this. When St Stephen was stoned to death he was radiant, he wasn't shaking with fright. Why am I afraid? So I went up to my room and shut the door and said, 'Lord, I don't understand this. I want to follow you, and even if it means that I am going to be killed I still want to follow you. But why the fear?'

When I said that, the fear went away. Then the Holy Spirit showed me that I was being tempted not to follow Christ if the cost was too great. And when I'd understood that, he showed me that during the last few months he had taken me through the three temptations of Jesus.

I was sitting there peacefully in my room enjoying the Lord's presence, when suddenly God spoke. He said: 'I cannot bless the church in this land, because the leaders of the church are not prepared to go the way of the cross.'

This was an enormous surprise to me. I didn't know anything about the church leaders. I didn't know who they were, or what they were up to. But I was very troubled by this remark, because I wondered what would happen to us all if God couldn't bless the church. And it was from this word from God that I thought we must pray, we must see what the Lord wants to do. How can we pray for the church? For church leaders? It was in the second half of the '60s that I got together with a couple of friends, on a weekly basis, to start praying and to seek the Lord's face. At first we prayed for ourselves and our families, but gradually God started to lead us out into bigger prayers for the nation and for the church, at first in our own nation, but gradually world-wide.

That same year, 1966, I was praying for a friend of ours. As I prayed, the Lord impressed on me his grief over this man. Though he was a Christian leader, he was resisting the Holy Spirit in his life. As I continued to pray for him, a strange thing started to happen to me. I started having labour pains and contractions, and feeling as though I were giving birth. I was very puzzled by this, and sought understanding, and two verses of Scripture came to my mind. The first was St Paul saying to the Galatians: 'I travail in birth again until Christ be formed in you,' and the second, a couple of months later, from Hosea 13 'The pangs of childbirth come from him, but he is an unwise son, for now he does not present himself at the mouth of the womb.'

Now this second verse of Scripture gave me quite something to think about because when my first child was due to be born, he was lying crooked inside me. It was a very long and difficult birth, because he was heading somewhere where there wasn't an exit. This had made me feel helpless and despairing, because I knew that however much I heaved nothing could possibly happen, as he couldn't get out. This had gone on for what seemed a very long time, until the doctor finally moved him, and then he was born and all was well. But now, several years later, the word, 'an unwise son who does not present himself at the mouth of the womb' was confirming my own natural experience, but now in relation to this man for whom I was praying.

At that time there was a man called Edgar Trout who travelled round the country speaking to different Christian groups. He came quite often to our home, and we would pray with him and I would share with him all the things that I didn't understand that were happening to me. When I told him about this word I had had, he said that it was a word of knowledge, and the Lord was saying something to me in a language that I would understand, and that I should keep it in my heart and in his own time the Lord would reveal it.

Well, life went on and I went on praying. I continued to have these labour pains from time to time for fourteen years, but they increased and accelerated and became much more frequent and intense after 1977. During our times of intercession in our group, the Lord would, time and time again, lead us to pray for the church. He would lead us into praying for situations in other countries, and there came a time when he said that he had been asking us to pray just for individual nations, but now he was going to show us things globally. Perhaps we would be praying for Angola, where there was a revolution, but always he would impress on us to pray for the church, pray for the Christians there, pray that people will stand, that they will learn to pray, that they will learn to live in the Spirit.

One day sometime in the late '70s, the Lord led us into a meditation on his Body. As we meditated, we were impressed with the fact that a head has one body, not two or three bodies. Shortly after this there was the 500th anniversary of Sir Thomas More's birth, and as part of the celebration there was a service in the Crypt Chapel of the House of Commons. Cardinal Hume, the Catholic Archbishop of Westminster, took this service, and it was the first time a Catholic had taken a service in the Crypt Chapel since the Reformation. The Methodist Lord Tonypandy, then Mr Speaker, was there, as were all the different denominations. But there was such as furore and row about a Catholic taking the service from some Members of Parliament, particularly from Northern Ireland. It was so painful and distressing. The truth was being affirmed that Jesus is the head of one body. But what a body! It was such a bad witness to the other MPs who are not Christians, who must have thought that if this was Christianity, who needed it!

One day as we were praying in December 1977, the Lord said, 'Now I am about to take the church through the way of the cross.' He impressed on us that we were to pray for the Archbishop of Canterbury and the clergy. We started to pray over the next few months, wondering in what way the Lord was going to do this. The next summer, 1978, there was the Lambeth Conference, the conference of Anglican bishops from all over the world. With my limited understanding I thought that as we'd been asked to pray for the Archbishop and clergy, that something dramatic was going to happen at the Lambeth Conference. I thought that if the head of the body (the bishops being the head of the Anglican body) went the way of the cross, the rest of the body would follow too. So we prayed like anything for that conference, and for the bishops. But nothing seemed to get born. And my labour pains went on. Of course later on I realized that I had been thinking only of the Anglican body and not the whole body of Christ.

Meanwhile something else was happening. In January 1978 the Archbishop called together what later became the Nationwide Initiative of Evangelism. This was a group of representatives of all denominations who met to consider how together they could evangelise the country. They formed an executive committee, originally of twelve people. As they wanted some women on it, I was invited as an Anglican, with a Catholic nun, to represent women. We started to meet in March, and we met for a whole day once a month, to pray and worship and discuss together, all different church traditions, to see what the Lord would do, and out of this came the organisation of an assembly at Nottingham in September 1980, to which 900 people came.

Early in that year, Michael and I had a free weekend. It was during our Northern Ireland period, and it was marvellous to have a weekend free of duty. I was most excited at the prospect. But there was to be no peace for me. I spent the entire weekend having labour pains, and I could scarcely sleep at night because of the contractions. So when it came to Monday, and our intercession group meeting, I just lay on the floor and wept. I was exhausted and miserable. 'Lord,' I complained, 'what is going on? I'm utterly fed up with this unwise son. I wish I understood what was going on. If you have an ordinary baby, you know what you are doing. It goes on for nine months and then that's it. And the labour doesn't last very long, just a few hours or maybe a day or two. But this has been going on for fourteen years. How much longer is it going on for? Am I going to be in labour for the next twenty or thirty years? And what is it anyway? I *think* it's a baby, and a disobedient son, but maybe it isn't. Maybe all this is just psychosomatic, and I'm just nuts.'

Then I calmed down and just wept. I said: 'Lord, it doesn't really matter if I do go on in labour for the rest of my life. If you explained it to me I probably wouldn't understand it, so it's not worth your while, I just love you anyway. It *would* be a help though if you could give us a clue about it, even if just to say that I'm nuts.'

Then the Lord gave us two clues. The first was the verses from Romans 8 about the whole creation groaning together for the revealing of the sons of God. And the second was from Isaiah 42 where he says: 'For a long time I have held my peace, I have kept still and restrained myself; now I will cry out like a woman in travail, I will gasp and pant.'

The more I thought about it, the more I thought that this baby was the 'One Body' baby – Jesus as the head of one body – and that it was due to be born during the assembly at Nottingham, when all these different denominations were gathered together.

I arrived at Nottingham feeling completely detached from the whole thing. I thought, one of two things is going to happen here this week. Either people are going to come with contrite hearts, wanting to see what the Lord will do, ready to die to themselves and their preconceived ideas, in which case a baby will be born. Or else it won't. People will come with hard hearts, and not want to see what God will do, in which case the baby will be still-born, or not born at all. In which case what will happen is that we will be wiped out as a nation. It will be like Sodom and Gomorrah.

However I expected that it would end in blessing and not cursing, because a few years previously as we had been praying, God had said, 'I have heard the prayers of my people, and I will bless this land.'

From the moment the assembly started on Monday I felt excited, as one could sense that people really meant business, and wanted to see what God would do. Then on Friday morning, before the main speaker, there were two short items. The first came from the Rev. Donald English, a Methodist and the chairman of the NIE. He gave an illustration of a human pyramid, in a gym class. There are four people at the bottom, then another three and then another two, and finally one at the top. It is essential in order for the pyramid to work properly, that all the people pull their weight. If one person slips the whole pyramid collapses. Then the Rev. Tom Houston, a Baptist, who was organising the assembly, gave a little talk about dying to oneself, which was essential for us if we were to go forward together.

As these two spoke it was as if the Holy Spirit was giving me a nudge. I was so excited, and I thought: is this for real? Am I really seeing what I think I'm seeing? What I think I'm seeing is the moment of birth: the unity of the body (the pyramid picture) going through the way of the cross (the dying bit). This was the head coming through into the resurrection life.

I happened to be sitting next to a Baptist Minister, the Rev. David Pawson, so I asked him what he thought of this. David was very excited, and said this was the prophetic word coming through for the first time in the NIE. On the other side of me was sitting a Catholic woman, Vivian Sewell, who is one of our little intercession group in London, and she had come to the conference in order to pray. The previous night she'd been asleep in bed and she woke at 2 a.m.; feeling that the Lord was asking her to pray she got up and went to the prayer room, where she prayed for one and a half hours. The whole time the focus of her prayers was about dying, and when Tom said his bit about dying, Vivian nudged me and said that that was what the Holy Spirit was wanting to do.

This to me was the most exciting moment. After fourteen years the baby had been born! The wondering and puzzling was over.

That evening we had a talk on the Holy Spirit by Fr Ian Petit. I had never heard him speak before, but a couple of days previously, as I had been praying for him, I had an impression of his talk as a clear mountain stream, cool and very refreshing, sparkling with lights, a stream of living water. As he spoke that evening his talk was just like that, and we all sat bathed in it. It was the quality of the resurrection life. This talk couldn't have happened earlier in the conference – only after the birth of the baby. It was as if the baby was coming out into the resurrection life, and this quality of life involved the whole body of Christ together, all denominations.

Again, one of our intercessors was praying, and twice God said to him, about the conference: 'You are seeking well, and you are speaking well. Now how about listening?' So I took this message to Donald English, the chairman, and on the Saturday morning he gave a superb address in which he said that we'd been doing a lot of talking, so now how about listening to the Holy Spirit, who might have things to say to us. So he kept us all quiet for ten minutes while we listened.

This is the quality of the resurrection life. In Romans 8: 14 we read: 'As many as are led by the Spirit of God, they are the sons of God.' And Jesus says, 'My sheep hear my voice'. He wants to communicate with us as we come away from our preconceived ideas and our old understanding, dying to ourselves, out into the resurrection life, saying, 'Lord, what do you want to do? How can we co-operate with you?'

It was a thrilling conference, and I just felt euphoric and elated. Those who have had babies know that that's how one sometimes feels after one has given birth to a baby. So now I thought, either I'm dreaming or this baby has been born.

The following Monday I shared this with our intercession group, and the Spirit witnessed with all of us that a new thing had happened, that a new little 'One Body' baby had been born in England, and was out in the resurrection life. And we all rejoiced and praised together, 'that a manchild had been born into the world.'

In 1981 I read an article by Clifford Longley in *The Times*. It was an assessment of the church, and he quoted the two dates, 1966 and 1980. He said that in 1966 everything was going down in terms of numbers: ordinands weren't coming forward for ordination; numbers were down in theological colleges; people weren't coming to churches for baptisms etc. In 1980 there was a whole upturn and now something different was happening. I was fascinated, because it was between those two dates that I had experienced my 'labour'.

The month after the Nottingham assembly, as we were praying, the Lord impressed on us Isaiah 11:1: 'There shall come forth a shoot from the stump of Jesse, and a branch shall grow out of his roots.' We had a picture of a frail little green shoot coming out of a tree.

Now I had always thought that this referred to Jesus, and of course it is Jesus in his earthly life, but it is also Jesus in his resurrection life. The stump is the churches, the structures, and this little shoot of new life, this frail little thing, is the new birth that has happened as the different denominations come together to worship. It is the life of Christ coming out of it, and it is the same thing as in Isaiah 53 where it talks about a tender plant coming out of dry ground.

The following March I was in Plymouth speaking to a Lydia Group, and I shared this picture of the baby, and the shoot coming from the stump. After my talk a woman came to me and said: 'In our group we had a picture of a babe in arms, and a stump of a tree with a shoot growing out over a pile of ashes. We didn't know what this picture meant, but there you are explaining the same picture.' It was a lovely confirmation in the Spirit that something was happening.

That evening we had a Prison Fellowship meeting, and just before the meeting a small group of us were praying – the Chaplain from Dartmoor prison, a couple of ex-prisoners, a couple of Lydia women and me. The men hadn't been at the afternoon meeting but now one of the ex-prisoners said, 'I've got a picture of a tree, and it's a huge and mighty tree, and its got masses of branches and masses of leaves, and God came along and he cut off all the branches and all the leaves and he left a stump and out of this stump was growing a new little shoot.' He added, 'I don't know what this means but this is what I'm seeing at the moment.'

And that was what we'd been talking about that afternoon! So it seems that God is doing a new thing, bringing together people from all over the country, bringing forth the 'One Body' baby as we die to ourselves, our preconceived ideas and emerge into the resurrection life: groups of people who want to worship God in spirit and in truth, not according to this structure or that structure, or this denomination or that denomination, but following his lead, and listening to him. This new little shoot is the life of Christ in the nation.

10

Two in one

The body of Christ is made up of different individuals grouped in various denominations, traditions and so on – all those who acknowledge Christ as their head, and want to be his disciples. And one of the most basic human groupings, one of the most significant cells in church life, is the married couple. Their 'one flesh' relationship, the two people as one relationship, is a picture of the community in unity, and of the Godhead itself – three in one.

Once in the early 1960s I was praying for a married couple who were friends of ours. As I prayed, I had a visual impression of a house, looking very nice on the outside. But then the breeze of the Spirit blew and shook the house to its foundations, and as the house shook it could be seen that there were lots of cracks in the walls, all neatly papered over. At about this time there were 'Anglican/Methodist Conversations' going on in church circles. As I considered this picture, relating to our friends' marriage, it was as if the Holy Spirit was saying: 'How can churches unite, and people from different traditions come together, when you don't yet know how to live together in the basic unit, which is marriage?'

In March 1978 I was in California. Jean Darnall was on a preaching tour which took her to many parts of the United States, and she had invited me to accompany her for three weeks as her travelling companion.

We had met in St Louis, spent an exciting few days in Oregon, come to Los Angeles for some speaking engagements, and now Jean was in Hawaii leaving me with friends in the Granada Hills.

On this particular March afternoon my friend Mary-Ellen drove me with her on a visit to her doctor, and I was left sitting alone in his waiting room. I sat there contentedly, enjoying the California sunshine, and not thinking of anything in particular, when suddenly I became aware of the Lord God speaking to me. 'I hate divorce,' he said. 'It is an abomination to me when people say "Praise the Lord" and "Hallelujah" and get divorced. It is just as much an abomination to me as when unborn foetuses are killed, and when Jews are put in a gas chamber. Why do you call me "Lord, Lord," and do not the things that I say?'

At the same time as this word, I had a visual impression of husband and wife as one flesh, one entity, and as they got divorced it looked like an amputation, the body was sawn in two and the limbs were left quivering and bleeding. Then as one partner remade his or her life, the other partner was left, cut off from the body, alive still but palpitating and bleeding. Then as I looked, I saw thousands of amputated limbs, all littering the body of Christ, looking rather like those heaps of bodies in photographs of concentration camps, only these heaps were alive and quivering. The Lord of Life was mutilated by divorces.

I sat aghast, with a terrible pain in my heart. The previous year I had spoken at some women's meetings in Washington, New York and Houston, Texas. I had been very grieved, while praying and talking with the women after the meetings, about how many had terrible marriage mix-ups and problems. I thought particularly of one woman who had held my hand and wept. She was struggling with her emotions. Her husband had left her and gone to live with another woman. She was longing to forgive him in order to be able to cope with her own life, but the thought of him sleeping with this other woman was more than she could bear, she was so jealous and bitter and resentful. All I could do was hold on to her and weep with her. Now I saw her as God saw her, an amputated, bleeding limb.

That evening Jean rang me. We were to meet next day at a women's luncheon, at which she was the guest speaker. She asked me if I would say a few words. I asked her what I should speak about. 'Say whatever God gives you to say. He is with you,' she said.

As I brushed my teeth the next morning I said, 'Lord, what would you like me to speak about?' The answer clearly came, 'Tell them what I told you yesterday.'

Jean and I had not compared notes. I did not know the subject of her talk. She spoke on marriage relationships from the life of King David. At the end she introduced me and asked me to speak. I told them what had happened to me the previous afternoon.

Jean later told me that a woman she counselled after the meeting told her she had been contemplating divorce, but was now going to work at putting her marriage together. God's word had acted powerfully on her.

I have belonged to a little intercession group now for over ten years. Each week during school term times we have met to fast and pray for the nation. Often we have come with preconceived ideas as to what we wanted to pray for, and each with our different thoughts. But as we have met to acknowledge Christ as Lord, to worship him, to ask for cleansing from our own thoughts and to ask him to show us how to pray, so the Lord has led us into totally unexpected areas of thought. 'Call unto me and I will answer thee and show thee great and mighty things which thou knowest not,' says the Lord, through Jeremiah the prophet. Each week has been an adventure. Some weeks it has been very hard work as we have put on the armour of God and united in spiritual warfare against the powers of darkness. Some have been times of deep refreshment and healing of wounds. Sometimes the Scriptures have been revealed to us in a new way, and we've searched them together, our hearts burning within us as the Lord showed us the relevance of his word to the situations we brought before him in prayer.

'My thoughts are not your thoughts, neither are my ways your ways.' Increasingly we have come to say, 'Lord, what do you think? What do you want to do in this situation? How can we help you?'

As we have prayed about marriages over the years: our own, our friends', the divorce laws, the discussion in Synod, he has taught us more and more about his purpose for marriage. Husband and wife are one unit. Through their life together and love for one another children are born. So in Scripture, Christ is called the bridegroom, and the church is the bride. Through the union of Christ and the believer, new birth is brought to the souls of others and more people born into the Kingdom. Marriage on earth is a visual aid to the relationship between our Lord and his bride. It is not surprising that the enemy has been so hard at work attacking and attempting to destroy marriages.

In the autumn of 1979 I was on a train travelling to Exeter in the West Country to speak to a Lydia Fellowship conference. The previous week, while asking for a message for these women, I had been brought to my knees in awe at the thought of God, holy, seated on his throne, and the words that were drawn from me were those of Isaiah: 'Woe is me, for I am undone, for I am a man of unclean lips and I dwell among a people of unclean lips.' As I pondered this cry, it was borne in on me that I should point to God's thoughts, as being quite different from our thoughts, and show that we were all, in our different ways, stuck in our own thoughts. Our carnal thoughts were like a huge bowl of cold porridge; people got stuck in them preventing them from being able to see God's perspective.

On the train I was thinking of the problem of homosexuality. Earlier that summer I had been walking down the Earls Court Road at closing time, and had been deeply grieved by the sight of so many gays pouring out of the pubs. My heart went out to them in their loneliness and confusion of identity, and I cried out to the Lord, 'What's to be done?' Now this autumn, the Church of England Report on Homosexuality had just been published, and as I read the reports of it in the Christian press, it seemed to me that it was totally stuck in carnal thinking, stuck as in a bowl of cold porridge.

As I prayed and thought and searched the Scriptures on the train my eye was drawn to Luke 16: 18: 'Whoever divorces his wife and marries another commits adultery. . . ' Deeply puzzled I considered this verse. 'What has this got to do with homosexuality, Lord?' Then as I puzzled, I seemed to receive the following understanding. God has made a pattern for mankind, and has given us his word and examples from nature, to teach us. When we ignore his revelation and teaching we make a mess. 'Where there is no vision the people perish.' (Prov. 29:18) There is no point in tackling the problem of homosexuality until first God's pattern has been looked at. Many heterosexual people have made just as much a mess of their lives as homosexuals. There are many, many people who think that they are married. According to man's carnal thinking, they are. But God doesn't think so: he thinks that they are living in adultery.

11

The day the rains came

The United Kingdom is not an island sufficient unto itself: it is part of a much bigger community. It is part of the European Economic Community, and it is also part of an even larger community, that of the Commonwealth, covering a quarter of the world's land mass.

I would like to share with the reader something about the Commonwealth, to ask for your prayers, so that together we can say, 'Lord, how would you like us to help you? How can we co-operate in what you are doing?'

In June 1981 Michael and I were invited by the Prime Minister to attend the Trooping the Colour ceremony from her stand on Horseguards Parade, behind 10 Downing Street. Now this was an enormous honour, and it was quite unlikely that we should have been invited. The reason that we were was that she had invited three widows of the Royal Ulster Constabulary from Fermanagh, with their children. They were women whose husbands had been killed by IRA terrorists, and we were there to escort them, as at that time Michael was a Minister of State in Northern Ireland.

It was the first time I had ever been to the Trooping the Colour ceremony, though I had seen it on TV of course. It was a marvellous sunny day, and when we went in we discovered that all the other guests in Mrs Thatcher's stand were the Commonwealth High

Commissioners from all over the world, with their families. The Australian and New Zealand High Commissioners were there, the President of Gambia, and High Commissioners of all the other countries, including the High Commissioner of Uganda whom I'd met before and through whom we'd been able to send vegetable seeds for growing food in the prison compounds in Uganda.

Well, we were sitting there in the sunshine; I had one of the women from Fermanagh on either side of me; it was the most superb and exciting thing to watch. The Queen's horse had been fired on in the Mall, on her way from the Palace, but we had no hint of that on Horseguards Parade. She arrived with perfect timing and in complete control, escorted by Prince Philip, Prince Charles, and the Duke of Kent. The marching was perfect, the bands of the Coldstream Guards, the Welsh Guards and the Irish Guards played superbly. As I sat there my heart was bursting with pride and excitement, and I thought how marvellous it was. And I could see that these High Commissioners were all excited too; this was something we all belonged to: the Monarchy, as the head of the Commonwealth, world-wide.

As I sat there, I said, 'Lord, why have you given me this treat? why am I here?' I felt as if the King of kings, our Lord, had suddenly scooped me up beside him, and that we were looking at something together, from his perspective – that I was on the edge of a revelation. And then I remembered something. And I thought, Oh, I can't cope with this, it's too big for me.

What I remembered was this. In 1965 Michael and I had been to a garden party at Buckingham Palace, one of the three annual parties which the Queen gives, and to which many people come. We were standing in a line, waiting for the Queen to come by, when it started to rain. As we stood there, quietly waiting, I had the impression that the Holy Spirit was trying to draw my attention to something. At that time I was learning about the gifts of the Spirit, things like the laying on of hands for healing, and Edgar Trout had said to us, 'If the Lord gives you an anointing for something, ask him "What is this for?" ' I thought maybe somebody was ill and the Lord would like to heal him, so I said, 'Lord, who is ill? What's this for?' I looked round, and I couldn't see anybody ill, so I thought, Well it must be something else, and asked again, 'Lord, what's it for?' All I could think about was the rain, and the thought shot through my mind that Elijah had asked for it not to rain, and it hadn't rained, and he'd asked for it to rain and it had rained. As I thought this, I heard what sounded like a man's voice saying out loud: 'The prayers of a righteous man availeth much.' I thought it was the man standing next to me who had said it, so I looked at him, but he wasn't saying a thing: he was just staring into space. So I said to the Lord: 'This is very extraordinary, Lord. I don't understand one thing about this. But if you want me to ask for it to stop raining, I'll ask for it to stop raining. So please will you make the rain stop.'

On the word 'stop', the rain stopped. It was as if somebody had switched off a tap. It didn't peter out: it just stopped. Everybody's umbrellas came down. The sky was dark grey, and people were commenting on how odd it was. Why had it stopped raining? Michael turned to me and said, 'How very peculiar. What's happened to the rain? It's stopped.'

I told Michael what had happened. He was so surprised. And so was I. We were both astonished. I hadn't used any faith; I hadn't necessarily believed that God was going to make it stop raining. It had all happened so fast, and almost as a reflex action I had just said, 'Lord, OK, I'll ask; please will you make the rain stop.' So now we agreed together, Michael and I, that I would ask for something specific, and this time exercise faith. It was now 4.40 p.m. and the garden party ended at 6.00 p.m. So I said to the Lord: 'Lord, seeing you've been so very kind as to do this, and seeing you've been so kind as to let me see you doing this, I'd like to ask you something. Please could you stop the rain until 6 o'clock. After six, let it rain as much as you like. But please, no rain till six. Thank you very much.'

So then we walked about the garden having tea and chatting to people. Three different people came up to Michael and said, 'Do you think it's going to rain?' and each time Michael said, 'It will rain after six, but it won't rain before six.' They all looked surprised at his answer to their rhetorical question!

At about 5.50 p.m. we decided to make for our car, so that we'd be in it when the rain came down. So we trotted up Birdcage Walk to the House of Commons where our car was parked. We arrived at 6.05 p.m. just as the rains came down. It simply poured—buckets of water, the sort of rain that jumps six inches off the pavement. As we shut the door of our little car I was shaking with fright. The fear of the Lord fell on me. I didn't dare look up, I was so afraid of God. I sensed his presence everywhere. This is how Noah must have felt when he got into his ark, and the rains came down.

For a long time I puzzled over this. What could this mean? Why had this happened? The more I thought about it over a period of time, the more I thought that this had something to do with the Queen and the Commonwealth. The reason I thought this was because amongst the guests at the garden party were the Commonwealth Prime Ministers, over in London for the Commonwealth Prime Ministers' Conference. I started praying for Rhodesia, which in 1965 had declared UDI. I felt, somehow or other, that God was bringing judgement on the Queen and Commonwealth.

I'd forgotten about this till now. Sixteen years later, here we were at the Trooping the Colour ceremony, and here was this brilliant sunshine, and the Queen and Commonwealth representatives. Prison Fellowship in England had just given vegetable seeds to be planted in the prison grounds in Uganda, for the prisoners to use for food: we felt seeds were a symbol of a new beginning and a new hope. We'd done this through the Ugandan High Commissioner. The Australian High Commissioner was there, and Prison Fellowship in Australia had just started; the New Zealand High Commissioner was there, and we were going to New Zealand in October because Prison Fellowship in New Zealand had just started. I started to shake and to tremble, and it was as if the Lord was impressing on me that he'd brought judgement on the

Commonwealth, but now he was going to start building up, from the ground floor up, blessing.
God is bringing forth justice to the nations. (Isaiah 42.1)

Sometimes one's attention is drawn to something by the way things happen. A couple of weeks after this Trooping the Colour ceremony somebody told me something about a little country called Belize. I had known nothing about this country, but apparently we had not had diplomatic relations with Guatemala for 150 years because of Belize, formerly called British Honduras. It's a tiny little country with a population of 145,000. We were protecting it because the people didn't want to be run by Guatemala, they preferred the British, but there they were in Central America.

The next day, our Prison Fellowship office received a circular letter from the United States saying, amongst other things, that someone in Belize had written asking to start Prison Fellowship there.

The following evening we were at a reception, and were talking to a Foreign Office minister, who started talking about Belize. He said that we were working towards giving it its independence that September, but he was fearful that before this happened there might be troubles, as there often seem to be troubles as countries become independent.

I thought then that perhaps the Lord would like people to pray for Belize. But perhaps more than that, that he would like us to pray for all the Commonwealth countries. The Lord is doing something mind-blowing and sensational world-wide. This is the impression I had at the Trooping the Colour. Jesus hasn't called us servants. He's called us friends. He's sharing with us his secrets and plans. Will you ask the Lord to show you, personally, how you can pray?

12

The work continues

One day, during the summer of 1981 I was praying about the direction Prison Fellowship in England should take. We had been going for just over two years and little groups were springing up round the prisons all over the country. I was chairman of the Trustees in England, and at that time, as we were still at an embryonic stage, chairman of the little executive group that met monthly to pray for our work and development.

Before our first conference in 1978, as I was walking along a beach in Spain during our summer holiday, the Lord had impressed on me that we should not publicise our work. Before the house could be built, the foundations had to be laid, and this was boring, unglamorous, unphotogenic work. He reminded me of the work of Nehemiah in rebuilding the walls of Jerusalem, and that when the enemy heard about it, they sought to destroy it. So we were to proceed quietly, without publicity.

As if to underline this instruction, during the first two and a half years of our existence, Michael held a ministerial post in Northern Ireland. During this time he had police protection. I was allowed to come and go as I pleased, without detectives, but I was not allowed to publicize my whereabouts. So I spoke to many little groups around the country, without any publicity. The group leaders knew I was coming and arranged meetings. And the people who came to those meetings were a small few who really meant business, those the Lord was calling to pray for people in prison.

But now, as I prayed, I had an impression of all these little groups as a growing army of soldiers, each in their different platoons, with the group leaders as platoon commanders. And I had the thought that what an army needs is a general. And a general needs lieutenants and captains and suchlike, so that between them they can work out a strategy. Because soldiers are not just people milling about; they are disciplined and trained, and can be called into action at a moment's notice.

'That's a great idea, Lord,' I thought. 'But who is this general?' Then came the thought, 'The general is Peter Timms.'

Peter Timms had been the Governor of Maidstone Prison, and had been in the prison service for twenty-nine years, as workshop instructor, prison officer, deputy governor and governor. He was the first prison governor to invite me into his prison, and in January 1979 I spent a day with him in Maidstone. The evening before that visit I had been having supper with a girl friend in our kitchen at home. We had, as it were, invited the Lord to join us for supper, and have fellowship with us. I asked him why I was going to Maidstone the next day, and what he would like me to do or learn there. Surprisingly, the Lord impressed on me that I wasn't there to do anything, but that he wanted me to meet a special friend of his, in Peter. 'You're in for a treat,' he said.

As Peter took me round the prison the next day,

introducing me to people as we passed them, prison officers and inmates alike, I was carrying on a running commentary in my thoughts to the Lord. 'I see what you mean, Lord. I'm so glad to meet this special friend of yours.'

In April of 1981 Michael and I had gone to lunch with Peter at Maidstone, and had asked him to write a paper for us, working out, through his knowledge of the prison system, how we could take seminars into the prisons, and bring prisoners out for training and discipling classes.

And then that summer Peter left the prison service, was ordained as a Methodist minister, and started work in the East End of London.

Later that year I went to see him and his wife in their new home. I tried very hard to think of something specific to ask him to do. But all I could think of to say in the end was, 'Here is this army, and you are the general.' He responded most surprisingly. 'I'll do anything you want,' he said.

Then he told me that about five years earlier he had woken in the night, and the Lord had impressed on him two things. One was that he was to leave the prison service and be ordained. And secondly, that he was to start a prison prayer fellowship. So from January 1982 Peter has been our executive chairman.

All this happened at a time when I felt the restraint on us was being lifted, and we were allowed to start publicizing. The little cells were growing and blossoming, with all sorts of creativity, people taking ex-prisoners into their homes, finding them jobs, writing to them, visiting, helping the families of prisoners, all in a grass-roots, low profile, unpublicised way, from the bottom up. Now we needed a more high profile approach.

By March 1984, we had been going for five years. Peter's paper, our Prison Fellowship Development Document, which was written in conjunction with the present Assistant Chaplain-General of Prisons, was sent to every prison chaplain and every prison governor in the country, and also to certain key people in the Home Office, asking for their comments and suggestions. Then it was re-written, to take in the new ideas suggested by different people, and early in 1983 sent out, with a covering letter from the senior chaplains in the Home Office, to all the prison chaplains, prison governors, Prison Fellowship group leaders; to all the bishops, Anglican and Catholic, and the heads of the denominations; and to all the principals of the theological colleges in the country.

Since that time much work has been done through training weekends, and regional conferences. Peter has collected a team called the National Leadership Group, and between them they have produced national guidelines for groups, seminars, training of volunteer teams, residential aftercare, finance, and many other aspects of the work. This year we are starting seminars in the prisons. And we have been enormously helped by having on our team a lovely young woman, Rita Nightingale, who spent three years of a twenty year prison sentence, for alleged drug smuggling in Thailand. Rita became a Christian while in prison, and was visited there by Kathryn Grant, of Prison Fellowship International. On being pardoned and set free she returned to England, and has been a member of our staff since 1981. Her book *Freed for Life* published two years ago, has been a best seller, and she has told her story of God's grace to many inmates, in many prisons, up and down the British Isles and in the United States.

Last summer, July 1983, Chuck Colson held a Prison Fellowship International Symposium, the first of what is hoped will be three-yearly events, in Belfast. Fifteen chartered countries were present, as were also representatives from seven other countries. The fellowship was deep and immediate. We were one family: black, white, yellow, brown, men and women of different denominations and church traditions, yet one in Christ, seeking to build up the body of Christ in the prison situation.

Looking through the Prison Fellowship Directory for 1984 one can see that of the fifteen chartered countries, eight of them are from the Commonwealth, and of the nine counries that are in the process of being chartered, six of them are Commonwealth countries.

The following is taken from *Notes on the Commonwealth* which I found in the Commonwealth Institute in London: 'The Commonwealth, unlike the United Nations, has no charter. It has, instead, a series of declarations to which all member countries voluntarily subscribe'.

The Declaration of Commonwealth Principles says:

> The Commonwealth of Nations is a voluntary association of independent sovereign states, each responsible for its own policies, consulting and co-operating in the common interests of their peoples and in the promotion of international

understanding and world peace. . .

We believe that international peace and order are essential to the security and prosperity of mankind. . .

We believe in the liberty of the individual, in equal rights for all citizens. . .

We recognize racial prejudice as a dangerous sickness. . .

We oppose all forms of colonial domination and racial oppression and are committed to the principles of human dignity and equality. . .

We believe that the wide disparities in wealth now existing between different sections of mankind are too great to be tolerated. . .

We believe that international co-operation is essential to remove the causes of war. . .

In pursuing these principles the members of the Commonwealth believe that they can provide a constructive example of the multi-national approach which is vital to peace and progress in the modern world. The association is based on consultation, discussion and co-operation. . .

The Commonwealth consists of forty-nine nations, and makes up a quarter of the world's population. It is a voluntary association and ideally is a reflection to us, in the secular world, of the interelation between members of the body of Christ, world-wide. It is however, no more than a reflection, and is made up of 'The kingdoms of this world' with, amongst other things, many different religions.

The body of Christ, however, is taken from out of the kingdoms of this world and is made up of those who are disciples of Jesus Christ, the King of kings and Lord of lords.

For the Holy Spirit to change the structures of society, and to build God's house according to God's holiness and righteousness, Christians need to come together to pray and ask God what he would have them to do to co-operate with him. And we need to work within the structures. The Commonwealth is influenced by parliamentary democracy, common law, the Anglican Church and the English language. Latin American countries are influenced by Spanish and Portugese culture and language, Roman Catholicism, Roman law. These links need to be taken into account when praying for revival and renewal and change. God the Holy Spirit is always at work renewing life.

In our praying, he showed us that the ground floor was the prison population and the people that the rest of society has cast off. Later he showed us that the next layer was the law. In England, groups of magistrates meet to pray, to see what God will show them. This is chiefly to do with the sentencing of offenders, but it is also to do with implementing God's justice. This is God's house that he is building. It has to be built according to his pattern and plan, with both men and women doing their part.

When I was invited to join the Executive Committee of the Nationwide Initiative of Evangelism I asked the Lord if he really meant me to do this. I didn't see myself as a committee person, and couldn't understand what would be the point of my going on it. The Lord gave me to understand something like this: the men are the head of the body, and the women the heart. A body doesn't operate properly if it is all head and no heart, nor if it is all heart and no head. Both are needed. Men and women have different functions, and different ways of apprehending truth, but both are needed.

And one last word to intercessors. Once, in the 1960s, I was deeply depressed, longing and aching for a ministry, feeling that life was passing me by and I was achieving nothing. Then one night, as I was just dropping off to sleep, quietly the Holy Spirit impressed on me a gentle word: 'When I was in prison you came to me.' I was totally surprised. Although this word came as balm to my spirit, encouraging me and making me feel less forlorn, I was conscious that I had never been inside a prison. So I said, 'Lord, when did I visit you in prison?' I reached for my Bible and looked up Matthew 25, and read 'Then shall the righteous answer. . . when saw we thee. . . in prison, and came unto thee?' Even more baffled and surprised I put down the Bible, feeling strangely comforted, but not understanding it at all. It was several years before I ever set foot in a prison.

Of course in our prayer imagination, we can enter any prison in the world, and visit Christ in the prisoners there. We have that verse, Matthew 25:36, on all our Prison Fellowship literature, to remind and encourage ourselves that it is Christ who beckons us into the darkest of the world's jails.

Will you co-operate with our Lord in building his house, from the ground floor up, by marching into every prison of the world in prayer?